Animal Wisdom

NATURE'S GUIDE TO A HAPPY LIFE

SAM HART

Illustrations by Lena Nikolaeva

summersdale

ANIMAL WISDOM

An Hachette UK Company
www.hachette.co.uk

Summersdale Publishers Ltd
Part of Octopus Publishing Group Limited
Carmelite House
50 Victoria Embankment
LONDON
EC4Y 0DZ
UK

www.summersdale.com

Printed and bound in China

ISBN: 978-1-80007-005-9

Substantial discounts on bulk quantities of Summersdale books are available to corporations, professional associations and other organizations. For details contact general enquiries: telephone: +44 (0) 1243 771107 or email: enquiries@summersdale.com.

Introduction

As humans, we think we're so smart, but look around: the animal kingdom has so much to teach us. They may not be able to speak our language, but the wisdom of the world's incredible creatures – from familiar four-legged friends to more exotic beasts – is staring us in the face. This book is full of tiny tips and helpful hints inspired by our friends in the great outdoors. May these ideas refresh your thinking, lift your spirits and help you to embrace the ways of nature for a happier life.

Take time to relax

In the midst of a busy life, we often forget to slow down. Make sure you take as much time as you can during your week to relax and unwind. It will improve your focus and you can return to your tasks feeling refreshed and ready to tackle anything.

Believe in yourself

We all have doubts from time to time, but we needn't let them hold us back. Remember all those times in the past when something you expected to go badly turned out well? Now start to channel this power of positive thinking and watch the magic happen.

Exercise regularly

It may seem like a lot of effort to get active when you're feeling down or tired, but exercise is a great way to recharge your batteries and lift your mood. It floods your body with endorphins, making you feel great, and helps you sleep better. Breaking a sweat is nature's way of cooling and calming you down.

Always do your best

You don't have superpowers, unfortunately, but you do have gifts of your own. As long as you can say you gave something your best shot, with the time and talents at your disposal, you'll never really fail. A little bit of courage and hope will always keep you afloat.

Get plenty of sleep

Rest is your body's way of refreshing and repairing itself – your limbs need a break after the day's adventures and your brain wants to dream. Be good to yourself by staying in the realm of slumber for as long as you need, so that you feel recharged and ready to rock when morning comes around.

Have confidence

Walk through life with your shoulders back and your head held high – in other words, carry yourself with confidence! Even if you're faking it, if you do it for long enough, soon you won't be pretending any more.

Stay hydrated

Your body needs water to achieve its best –
after all, that's mostly what it's made of! Water
is good for your skin, your brain and your
energy levels, to name just a few benefits,
so keep a glass or bottle of the clear stuff on
hand throughout your day as a reminder to
sip regularly.

Stretch

You were not made to stay still all day. When you've been sitting in the same position for too long, your body may start to complain with aches and twinges. Every 20 minutes or so, get up and stretch out your arms and legs, breathing deeply and enjoying the release of tension. Learning yoga works wonders as well.

Enjoy the sunshine

Sunlight is good for us, boosting our bodies' levels of vitamin D and putting us in a good mood. Try to get out into the sun for at least 15 minutes a day and you'll be beaming in no time (and don't forget to use your sunscreen as necessary).

Dare to be different

The world would be so boring if we were all identical. Good job we're not! Your unique traits are your real strengths and playing to those will make you deeply happy in the long run. Don't try to be something you're not, and don't let anyone tell you who you should be; let your true nature point the way.

Make time for family

Even if its members don't always get along perfectly, being part of a family, or having a "village" of people to turn to, can be one of life's biggest blessings. Hopefully you can draw on the love and support of your family when you need it, and you can offer them the same. Stay in touch as much as you can to keep the bonds between you healthy and strong.

Ask for help

Nobody can truly go it alone. When you're struggling to solve a problem or get through a hard time, you'd be surprised how many people around you are willing to help, in whatever way they can. Let go of any misplaced sense of shame or failure and reach out. Being honest, out loud, is the crucial first step in getting back on track.

Embrace teamwork

We're always part of something bigger, and when we work with others, we can achieve great things that we couldn't achieve alone. Wherever you are in life, play your role passionately, help the people around you diligently and enjoy the fruits of your success as a team. The best endeavours will always be collective.

Go slowly

They say that slow is smooth and smooth is fast, meaning that you get things done in less time if you don't rush them (if you're hasty, you end up spending extra time fixing avoidable mistakes). So ease off the throttle whenever you can: take a breath, take a moment and then resume your mission with calmness and care.

Eat plenty of fruit and veg

Your diet is literally your life force, so try to make sure that not everything in it is beige and deep-fried! You need the goodness of plant power, bursting with fresh flavours and colours, every day. All those vitamins and minerals will keep you bounding happily through life.

Make time for fun

Play time is never wasted time. You need to take regular breaks from your work, even if it's just for a few minutes at a time. Taking your mind off difficult tasks and doing something creative or frivolous, purely for the enjoyment of it, will stop you from burning out. Amusing yourself is actually caring for yourself.

Try new things

It's called the comfort zone for a reason: it feels so nice to stay there. But remember that everything you love now was once new and unfamiliar, so stay open to new experiences, people, places and ideas. You might just find that life is more charming and colourful when you embrace a bit of change.

Make
your home
your own

Your environment influences the life you lead and the thoughts you have. So, wherever you live, whether it's a temporary spot or somewhere you want to stay put, make an effort to keep your home tidy and organized, and find ways to decorate and beautify your living space to keep yourself feeling comfortable and content.

Take care
of yourself

Good hygiene and grooming habits obviously help you stay healthy, but they are psychologically important too. You'll think of yourself as a more capable and confident person when you're looking and feeling fresh. Indulge in a little self-care every day and your mood will begin to glow to match your outward appearance.

Dance!

Life is one big dancefloor, so don't waste the opportunity to throw some shapes. Dancing is great exercise and we all know how feel-good music can lift our spirits. Even if you're just cooking in the kitchen with the radio on, shaking your hips to a killer tune does wonders for your sense of well-being.

Enjoy a treat

When life gets busy, it's the small, simple moments of bliss that get sacrificed first. To keep yourself motivated and rewarded, give yourself little treats over the course of your day or week. A relaxing bath is truly something to savour after you've had a long day, and a favourite meal at the end of a busy week is the perfect incentive to power through.

Believe
and achieve

Never limit your imagination and aspirations: dream big first, and then take the patient, incremental steps to realize that dream. Step by step, strand by strand, you can weave together something wonderful that you can be truly proud of. It starts with you at the centre of it all.

Be kind to others

It's a tough world out there at the best of times, so anything you can do to make it easier for others is always worthwhile. You never know what someone else is going through, but by being kind to everyone you encounter, you can make a real difference. You'll benefit from the positive vibes as well, so it's smiles all round.

Listen more

Silence is golden, and it's needed in order to really listen, learn and understand where someone else is coming from. We often miss what other people are saying because we're too busy talking on or waiting for our turn to speak. Try saying less and leaving space in any conversation for richer interactions.

Look out for your friends

When your friends are in trouble, you've got to be ready to offer whatever support or advice is called for. It's not just the right thing to do: your kindness will be remembered, and it's sure to be returned when it's your turn to face adversity. But don't wait for a crisis for the opportunity to be a good friend – be one every day. Check in with your pals whenever you can with the sole motivation of wanting the best for them.

Travel when you can

Life goes by quickly, so you can miss out on a lot if you spend most of it in the same spot. Whenever you have the chance to visit a new place, either in your own country or abroad, go for it. Memories and a greater appreciation of the wider world are far more valuable than the money you would save by staying put. Adventure awaits.

Take deep breaths

If you're stressed and taking lots of quick, shallow breaths, you're not getting all the oxygen your body craves. Pause what you're doing and slowly inhale some deep lungfuls of air through your nose, breathing out through your mouth just as calmly. It's an instant reset and a chance to be mindful in the present moment.

Don't follow the crowd

Trends aren't bad, but they can stifle your individuality. And if you have to fake enthusiasm for something you don't actually like, it will begin to weigh on you. Stay true to your genuine principles and preferences. Not everyone will agree with you, but you'll be more authentic and at peace with the life you lead.

Allow yourself to be vulnerable

Acting tough, and saying we're fine when we're really not, is something we all do from time to time. But there's no shame in opening up to someone you trust and expressing the emotions you may have been bottling up for a while. Letting it out is so much healthier than keeping it in.

Speak out!

It's always good to listen, but there are times when it's important to say something. It may feel uncomfortable, especially if you're in a group situation and you're going against the grain, but respecting and valuing yourself means sharing your opinion. Like emotions, honest thoughts are best expressed openly.

Make the most of your opportunities

Luck plays a big part in most people's lives. Sometimes it will just keep raining and there's nothing you can do but weather the storm. Yet there will be days when fortune smiles on you in a big way, and that's when you need to be ready. Help luck along by combining it with your own hard work and dedication – success is sure to follow.

Dress for success

It's no secret that our clothes affect how others treat us. It may not be right or fair, but it's true. What's also true is that our clothes affect how we feel about ourselves, so double up on the impact of your outfit by wearing garments that make you feel and look great in both your professional and personal life. Show your true colours.

Play to your strengths

It's impossible to be good at everything, so don't beat yourself up if you come up short when you tackle new tasks. Always remember that you can do some things better than anyone else, and that it's okay to focus on the areas where you excel. Make every effort to find and expand these competencies, while being proud of your finest talents.

Only own what you need

Less is more. The essentials of a good life are much less numerous than we might think – and those essentials are often not very expensive at all. Ask yourself honestly if you need everything you currently possess, and whether you truly need that new purchase you've been thinking about. Both your soul and the environment will benefit from being burdened with less unnecessary stuff.

Adapt to new situations

Your tried-and-tested methods may have worked up to this point, but something unexpected is always around the corner and you need to be ready to leap into action. Stay flexible in your approach and you'll soon hit upon the best way to handle any unfamiliar situation.

Stay organized

Admin can seem like such a chore, but look at it as a gift to your future self. If you do the work now, you'll get to enjoy the tranquillity that comes from having all your stuff sorted. A little bit of tidying up on a regular basis keeps things from descending into chaos too; if you find a place for everything, you'll never curse yourself again for mislaying something important.

Live in the moment

The past is gone, for better or worse, and the future is just a big unknown, but here in the present moment is where life really happens. Don't miss out on the joys of what's going on right now: embrace what all your senses are experiencing, let go of yesterday and tomorrow, and just be.

Stay chilled

Put everything into a healthy perspective. Most of the things that upset us today will soon disappear and leave little or no trace. Ask yourself if your current concern is worth stressing over. Do what you can to improve things, but accept what you can't. You can develop a healthy kind of zen attitude this way, and life should start to feel more of a breeze.

Love yourself

You may not hear it enough, so say it aloud to yourself: you're incredible! Be your own best friend and loudest cheerleader by banishing pesky doubts with pure, unconditional love for who you are. Forgive yourself, value your worth and show everyone that you're unstoppable.

Stay curious

The world is a vast and fascinating place and there's so much to see, learn, taste and experience. Keep your mind and your heart open to all of it. You don't need to climb every mountain or master every language, but never stop asking questions or exploring new perspectives. Forget about your bank balance: the more you take from life, the richer you get.

Form
good habits

It takes time and practice to fashion anything of worth and durability. Good habits are no different: you have to put in the effort early on, but once they're established it becomes second nature to keep them up. Know what your goal is, figure out the time and materials you'll need to achieve it, and then get to work.

Be bold

Playing it safe has its uses, but the thrill of striving for new heights can be very rewarding. You needn't go crazy, but a certain amount of uncertainty is good for us. Life is more interesting and exciting if everything is not always guaranteed. When the moment arises, be ready to pounce.

Agree to disagree

We love it when others agree with us, but that's not always possible. However justified you think you are on any particular point, you won't convince everyone. Accepting that others see the world differently will save you a lot of hassle in the long run, and being less dogmatic in your approach may even help you find some valuable common ground.

Stay humble

When you think you've got it all figured out, you're asking for trouble. Don't get too complacent, even when you're engaging with others who have less experience than you: they might know something you don't. Remember that you were once in their position. Try to pass on what you know and be ready to acknowledge all the things you don't.

Be positive!

Whatever you choose to do, wherever you choose to go, be positive. It's a habit like any other, so find the good in any situation, however gloomy it may seem on the surface, and really dwell on that. Keep doing this and you'll brighten your own life as well as the lives of those around you. You'll have irresistible charisma and an anything-is-possible attitude in no time.

Do what you love

It sounds so simple, but it's so true. None of us are getting any younger, so we're best off spending our valuable time on the things we're actually passionate about. Yes, that's often easier said than done, but there's always something you can do, a step you can take, to begin realizing your dreams. Start today. No, start right now!

If you're interested in finding out more about our books, find us on Facebook at **Summersdale Publishers**, on Twitter at **@Summersdale** and on Instagram at **@summersdalebooks**.

www.summersdale.com